T0055925

Creative Clarinet Duets

26 stylish duets for beginners

Kellie Santin

Cheryl Clark

OXFORD
UNIVERSITY PRESS

Dear Student,

Creative Clarinet Duets is a fabulous collection of 26 stylish duets that encourage beginner students to enjoy making music with other players both inside and outside of lessons. It is intended to be used alongside the first book in the series, *Creative Clarinet,* and the duets follow the progression of that book. There are helpful references to the corresponding chapters at the start of each piece.

All of the duets have their own backing track included on an accompanying CD. These offer the player an authentic experience of performing within an ensemble.

This is the second book in the *Creative Clarinet* series and it is followed by a third, *Creative Clarinet Improvising,* which expands on the skills introduced in books one and two.

Thank you for choosing *Creative Clarinet Duets*. We wish you many hours of happy music making!

Kellie Santin Cheryl Clark

Contents

Title	Creative Clarinet Chapters	Page	Track
Let's go	1–3	5	1
Equality	1–3	5	2
Taking it to the limit	1–3	6	3
Blast from the past	1–3	6	4
Mind the gap	1–5	7	5
Two's company	1–5	7	6
Jet lag	1–5	8	7
Cutting edge	1–5	8	8
Craving calypso	1–8	9	9
It's an illusion	1–8	10	10
Elizabeth	1–10	11	11
Put on your red shoes	1–10	12	12
The happening thing	1–10	13	13
Secret agent shuffle	1–13	14	14
Anyone for tennis?	1–13	15	15
In the meantime	1–13	16	16
Empty cupboards	1–15	17	17
Moving right along	1–15	18	18
Squeaky clean	1–15	19	19
Never say never	1–18	20	20
Excess baggage	1–18	22	21
Cool bananas	1–20	24	22
Under cover	1–23	26	23
Hot off the press	1–23	28	24
Gone troppo	1–25	30	25
And the winner is . . .	1–25	32	26

A tuning note (B) is located on track 27

Getting started

Playing along with the CD

- Tune up using the tuning note located on track **27**. The tuning note is **B**.
- Both parts are played on the CD. The top line is found on the left channel, and the bottom line is found on the right channel.
- When you are confident at playing your part, pan left or right (using the balance control on your audio equipment) and mute the part that you are playing. In this way, you can play along with either part as a duet.
- Remember to listen closely to the count-in at the beginning of each tune.
- Count the rests accurately.
- Most importantly, HAVE A GREAT TIME!

Chapters 1–3

1 Let's go

Kellie Santin

Chapters 1–3

2 Equality

Kellie Santin

Chapters 1–3

3 Taking it to the limit

Cheryl Clark

Chapters 1–3

4 Blast from the past

Cheryl Clark

Chapters 1–5

5 Mind the gap

Kellie Santin

Chapters 1–5

6 Two's company

Kellie Santin

Chapters 1–5

7 Jet lag

Cheryl Clark

Chapters 1–5

8 Cutting edge

Cheryl Clark

Chapters 1–8

9 Craving calypso

Kellie Santin

Chapters 1–8

10 It's an illusion

Chapters 1–10

11 Elizabeth

Chapters 1–10

12 Put on your red shoes

Cheryl Clark

Chapters 1–10

13 The happening thing

Cheryl Clark

Chapters 1–13

14 Secret agent shuffle

Kellie Santin

Chapters 1–13

15 Anyone for tennis?

Cheryl Clark

Chapters 1–13

16 In the meantime

Kellie Santin

Chapters 1–15

17 Empty cupboards

Kellie Santin

Chapters 1–15

18 Moving right along

Cheryl Clark

Chapters 1–15

19 Squeaky clean

Cheryl Clark

Chapters 1–18

20 Never say never

Kellie Santin

21
mf
mf
26
1.
2.
p
p
31
mf
mf
(straight quavers)
p
p
37
(straight quavers)
f
f
43
mp
mp
(straight quavers)

Chapters 1–18

21 Excess baggage

Kellie Santin

25
29
Majestically
f
f
33
Swing
mp
mp
37
41
mf
mf
45
ff
ff

Chapters 1–20

22 Cool bananas

Cheryl Clark

17
mp
mf
mf
mp
mf
mp
21
mp
mf
mf
mp
mf
25
f
f
29

Chapters 1–23

23 Under cover

Kellie Santin

21
mf
mf
f
f
25
f
f
29
mp
mp
33
37
41

Chapters 1–23

24 Hot off the press

Cheryl Clark

21
mp
mp
25
mf
f
29
f
33
f
37

Chapters 1–25

25 Gone troppo

Cheryl Clark

21
mf
mf
25
29
mp
mp
33
mf
mf
37
41
mf (1st time)
f (2nd time)
mf (1st time)
f (2nd time)

Chapters 1–25

26 And the winner is . . .

Kellie Santin